The Twins Go Bowling!

This book has been written specifically for Aidyn Dwayne Durr.
Copyright © 2018
Published by Gifted Genie Publishing
Madison Al 35757

Ashton and Aidyn Durr

Aidyn and his brother Ashton do everything together.
They take pictures together…

They wait for the bus together…

They even travel together…

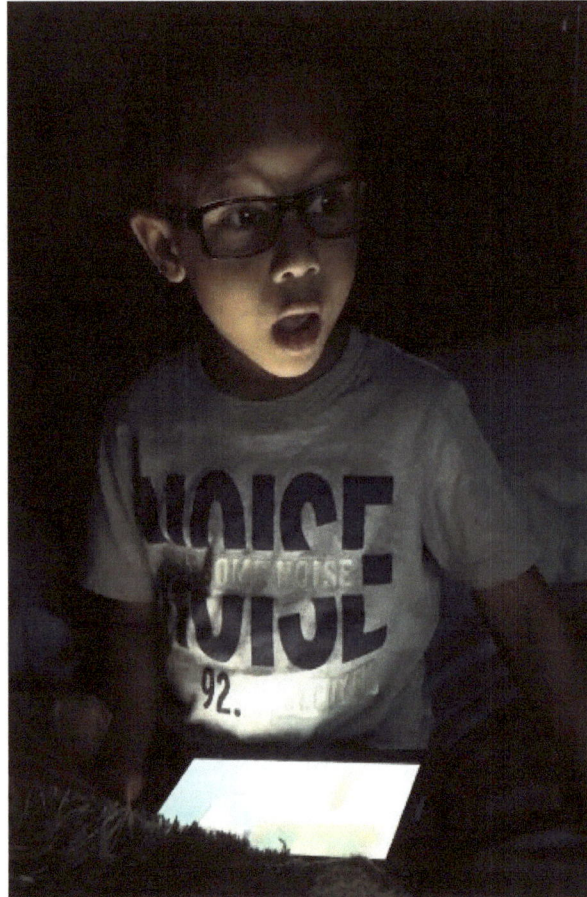

One night, while watching cartoons, Aidyn saw a commercial about bowling. "Ashton! This looks like fun. Want to go bowling?" he asked. Ashton looked up from his tablet.

"What? Aidyn, what's bowling?"

"I just saw it on television. Bowling is when you roll a ball and knock down stuff. Want to play?"

"What kind of stuff do we knock down? I don't want to

get in trouble Aidyn."

"You won't get in trouble Ashton." Aidyn got some
plastic cups from the backyard.

He stacked them up at the end of the hallway. "Let's play Ashton. I'll show you how. I'll get the ball", said Aidyn.

"I got the ball, I'm ready to play!" yelled Aidyn. Ashton came running into the hallway. "Wait a minute! I will show you how it's done", replied Aidyn.

Aidyn and Ashton stood side by side. "Watch what I do", said Aidyn. Aidyn rolled the ball down the hallway towards the cups.

The ball rolled and rolled until it
hit the cups!

Some of the cups fell down!

"That's how you do it. Give it a try Ashton!"

"Do I have to knock down all the cups?" asked Ashton.
No, but if you do that's called a strike
and that's really good!

Ashton picked up the ball and walked back to the end of the hallway while Aidyn stacked the cups again.

Ashton looked nervous. "Take a deep breath and then roll the ball, said Aidyn. You're going to do fine." Ashton took a deep breath, closed his eyes and rolled the ball. The ball rolled and rolled and…

All the cups fell down!
You got a strike! Said Aidyn!
Wow!

The boys jumped up and down!
"This is so much fun.
I want to play some more", yelled Ashton.

Looking at the clock on the wall Aidyn replied,
"We can't. Remember, our movie is starting soon.
Maybe tomorrow brother" said Aidyn.
"Yeah, said Ashton. Maybe tomorrow…"

The boys ran and got their
sleeping bags. They settled in
to watch their movie.

"Thanks for showing me how to bowl Aidyn.
It was fun," said Ashton as he turned the
volume up on the movie.

"You're welcome brother," replied Aidyn.

Movie Time!

Ashton and Aidyn do everything together!

The End

Want to enjoy another story about
the twins?
Check out *The Twins Go Fishing*.

You can find it on Amazon!

Do you have a child who has an amazing imagination for stories?
You are not alone. I write books for my grands all the time.
However, what I have learned is that their love of books
also includes creating stories of their own to share with others.
I founded a non- profit organization, Every Child Has a Story
that has a program dedicated to youth writers like Ashton and Aidyn.
It's called The Writers Vibe.

To learn more about Every Child Has a Story and
The Writers Vibe you can visit the website.
www.everychildhasastory.org

Bowling Word Search

```
H N S J S A H M Z I F J O F B
X Y H N O E I H V Z K Z J R L
M D T F K S N I P W J H W T G
J N I A X W V H X P O O B O O
Y Z B T P L V J K F E P C H A
G U O N J E T U E T M N N C F
E I W I V Y H D D Y U O L V E
L A L W J E W S K Z C C K X S
H X L L K L N K I T V Y L I P
P W H I K L U G K T L C Z O P
Z S R T R O P H Y B E L S B Y
R T H M H X V V A E X E O E B
S L H O Z S S L X X R T K R A
S S J Q E Q L X L U F J Q S O
K L Q P V S V C W R U X J G S
```

BALL   TROPHY   PINS   STRIKES
BOWL   WIN   ROLL   SHOES